First Step in
English
Discussion
2
Workbook

Contents

Building Vocabulary

A. Match the words with the pictures.

a.

b.

c.

d.

e.

f.

1. magazine _____e_____   **2.** backpack _____   **3.** baseball cap _____

4. alarm clock _____   **5.** picture _____   **6.** laptop _____

B. Practice the conversation with your partner. Then ask and answer the questions about other things in the pictures above.

A: Is there a _____magazine_____ in the picture?

B: Yes, it is.

A: Where is it?

B: It's _____on the TV_____.

C. Match the words and meanings. Draw a line between the word and its meaning.

WORD

MEANING

1.

bedroom

a. the bottom surface area inside a building

2.

build

b. a tame animal kept in the home

3.

floor

c. a room for sleeping

4.

pet

d. to make something by putting pieces together

D. Read the below sentences and choose the correct answers.

1. Yuna Kim will perform in a *charity* ice show. In this sentence *charity* means
   (a) an organization that gives money, food etc. to those who need it
   (b) to please someone very much, or make them think you are very attractive

2. People say that our house has a *ghost*. In this sentence *ghost* means
   (a) a town that is now empty because people no longer live there
   (b) the spirit of a dead person

A. Read and answer the questions.

Hello, everyone!

This is my bedroom. That is my green bed. It's very lovely, isn't it? Can you see the pink pillow? It's on my bed. I like it very much. The night table is beside the bed. It's brown. And an alarm clock is on the night table. It's pink and purple. Oh, this is my desk. It's blue. There is a laptop computer on my desk. I like to use the computer very much. I often use it to do my homework. My books are under the desk. The desk is next to the chair. My chair is blue, too. Ah, my baseball cap! It's on my chair. I like my bedroom very much.

1. Where is the night table?

(a) next to the bed   (b) behind the bed   (c) near the desk

2. Is the alarm clock on the night table?

(a) No, it isn't.   (b) Yes, it is.   (c) I don't know.

3. Where is the laptop computer?

(a) on the desk   (b) behind the desk   (c) near the desk

4. Is there a baseball cap under the chair?

(a) Yes, there is.   (b) We don't know.   (c) No, there isn't.

B. Look at the picture and write answers.

1. Q: How many floors are there?

A: There are _____ .

2. Q: How many rooms are there?

A: There are _____ .

3. Q: What rooms are on each floor?

A: The first floor has _____ .

There are a bathroom and _____

on the second floor.

Super Writing 1

A. Look at the pictures and write sentenses as in the example.

1.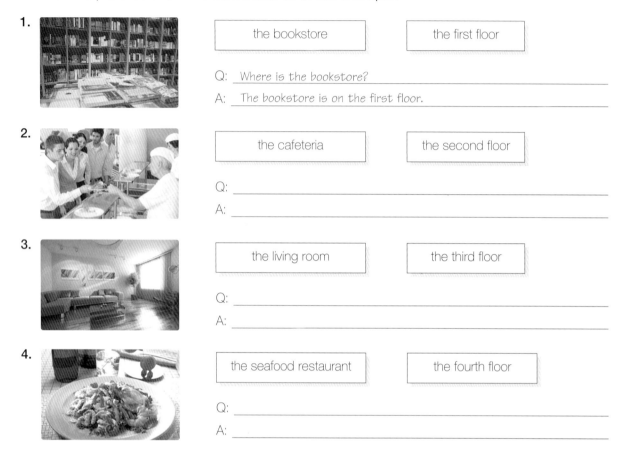

   | the bookstore | the first floor |

   Q: Where is the bookstore?
   A: The bookstore is on the first floor.

2.
   | the cafeteria | the second floor |

   Q: _____
   A: _____

3.
   | the living room | the third floor |

   Q: _____
   A: _____

4.
   | the seafood restaurant | the fourth floor |

   Q: _____
   A: _____

B. Look at the example and write sentences in the same way.

1.

   | pillows | on the sofa |

   ⇨ There are pillows on the sofa.

2.

   | math books | under the bed |

   ⇨ _____

3.

   | golf clubs | in my bedroom |

   ⇨ _____

Super Writing 2

- 1~3 Unscramble the words to make sentences.
- 4~7 Sentence Transformation. / N(Negative) / Q(Question) / T(Tense)

1.

they   at a charity soccer game   in 1997   .   met

⇨ _____

2.

Beckingham Palace   named   the press   .   their house

⇨ _____

3.

baseball cap   ?   where   my   is

⇨ _____

4.

You live in a house or an apartment. (Q)

⇨ _____

5.

You seem to like your new house. (T - Past)

⇨ _____

6.

I saw the ghost in the dining room. (N)

⇨ _____

7.

If you saw a ghost in your home, what would you do? (T - Future)

⇨ _____

Super Speaking!

A. Listen to the conversation between two people. Then answer the questions. While you listen, you can take notes. ● Track 5

Listening Notes

	Prepare ●··	Speak ●··
1. Does the man live in an apartment?	(5 seconds)	(10 seconds)
2. What did he do in the garden last Saturday?	(5 seconds)	(10 seconds)
3. Where did he see the ghost?	(5 seconds)	(10 seconds)

B. Look at the example and practice with a partner. Use the words below or invent your own. (Then change roles and practice again.)

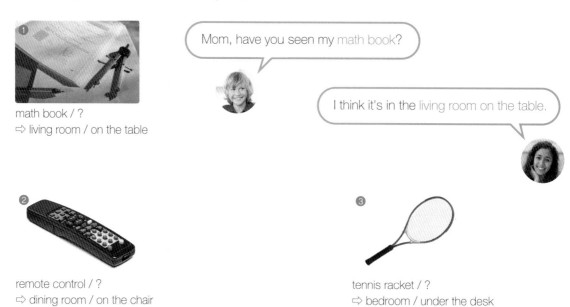

math book / ?
⇨ living room / on the table

Mom, have you seen my math book?

I think it's in the living room on the table.

remote control / ?
⇨ dining room / on the chair

tennis racket / ?
⇨ bedroom / under the desk

Grammar Focus 1

● **Prepositions of Place: in, on and under**

- Prepositions of place show where something or someone is situated.

They are in the tent.   My sister is on the bed.   The briefcase is under the table.

Grammar Focus 2

● **There Is(Are) + Subject**

- We use *there is/are to* say that something or someone exists in a particular place. To make a negative sentence, we put *not* after the verb be.

There are apples in the basket.

Q: Are there any eggs in the basket?
A: No, there aren't.

A. Write the complete sentences. (N: negative / Q: question)

1. There is a table in the kitchen.   ⇨ N: *There isn't a table in the kitchen.*

2. There is a telephone on the night tale.   ⇨ Q: _____

3. There are buses on the street.   ⇨ N: _____

4. There are five floors in this building.   ⇨ Q: _____

B. Read and make answers as in the example.

1.

the car

Q: Are they on the sofa?

A: No, they aren't. They are in the car.

2.

the balcony

Q: Is she standing behind the door?

A: _____

3.

the sea

Q: Is the boy on the boat?

A: _____

4.

the school bus

Q: Are the children at the bus stop?

A: _____

Super Speaking

● Look at the example and practice with a partner. Use the words below or invent your own. (Then change roles and practice again.)

a man / behind the door / ?
No ⇨ in front of

Is there a man behind the door?

No, there isn't. He is in front of the door.

a woman / under the bench / ?
No ⇨ on

a teddy bear / on the bed / ?
No ⇨ next to

Building Vocabulary

A. Draw lines to make verb phrases. Then use the past verb form to complete the sentences.

1. play •   • a. my homework   I _did my homework_____ last night.

2. watch •   • b. by plane   They _____ last Sunday.

3. clean •   • c. delicious food We _____ at the restaurant.

4. go •   • d. TV   I stayed home and _____.

5. do •   • e. the house   She _____ last weekend.

6. travel •   • f. soccer   Peter _____ with his friends.

7. have •   • g. to the movies They _____ yesterday.

B. Circle the correct words and fill in the blanks.

1.

Jason _____ for a bicycle ride on Sunday.

       (went / rode)

2.

On Saturday morning she _____ late.

       (swam / got up)

3.

This food smells bad. We'd better _____ it.

       (eat / throw)

11

C. Match the words and meanings. Draw a line between the word and its meaning.

WORD

MEANING

1.

magazine

   a. to visit a place on a tour

2.

museum

   b. a glass or plastic container for liquids

3.

bottle

   c. a thin book containing articles, fiction, photographs, etc.

4.

tour

   d. a building where many valuable and important objects are kept so that people can go and see them

D. Read the below sentences and choose the correct answers.

1. We *visited* our friends in town. In this sentence *visit* means
   (a) to go and see a person or place
   (b) someone who goes and sees a person or place

2. The actors' performances didn't come up to my *expectation*. In this sentence *expectation* means
   (a) good at something because you have done it before
   (b) the belief that something will happen

A. What did David and Sandra do last Saturday? Write sentences as in the example.

1.

play / basketball

⇨ Sandra played basketball last Saturday.

2.

ride / his bicycle

⇨ _____

3.

talk / on the phone

⇨ _____

4.

clean / the house

⇨ _____

B. Complete the conversations. Choose (a), (b) or (c).

What did you do last weekend?

(a) Umm, I spent most of the time at the skating rink.
(b) What did you do?
(c) Oh. No, I was too tired.

1. So how was your weekend, Bob?

   (a) Oh, I went to see that new horror movie downtown.

   (b) Yes, It's much warmer now than it was this morning.

   (c) It was great. We had a family get-together.

2. Did you go anywhere interesting last summer?

   (a) Yes, I did. I stayed home yesterday.

   (b) Yes, I did. I went to the beach almost every day.

   (c) Yes, I did. I studied for the chemistry test.

Super Writing 1

A. Look at the example. Make conversations as in the example.

1.

| stay home and watch TV | bake some cookies |

A: What did you do over the weekend?
B: _Oh, I stayed home and watched TV._ What did you do?
A: _I baked sonme cookies._

2.

| clean my room | go to the zoo |

A: What did you do over the weekend?
B: _____ What did you do?
A: _____

3.

| play tennis with my dad | go fishing at a lake |

A: What did you do over the weekend?
B: _____ What did you do?
A: _____

B. Look at the example and write sentences in the same way.

1.

| I | go to the movies | Saturday night |

⇨ _I went to the movies on Saturday night._

2.

| my grandfather | cook me *bulgogi* | Sunday afternoon |

⇨ _____

3.

| Nancy | study Chinese | Sunday morning |

⇨ _____

Super Writing 2

- 1~3 Unscramble the words to make sentences.
- 4~6 Sentence Transformation. / S(Statement) / T(Tense)
- 7~8 Blank Completion

1.

| and read | . | breakfast | ate | I | a magazine |

⇨ _____

2.

| with my younger sister | of Art History | . | to | I | the Museum | went |

⇨ _____

3.

| with us | . | I | that | was | sorry | couldn't come | mom |

⇨ _____

4.

| watched | I | action movie | . | the latest |

⇨ _____

5.

Do you have enough free time on the weekend? (T - Past)

⇨ _____

6.

Did Jessica listen to K-pop music yesterday? (S)

⇨ _____

7.

Q: _____

A: No, I didn't watch TV yesterday. I helped my mom.

8.

Q: What _____?

A: I'm going to go fishing with my father this Saturday.

Super Speaking!

A. Listen to the conversation between two people. Then answer the questions. While you listen, you can take notes. ⊙ Track 15

Listening Notes

	Prepare ●●●	Speak ●●●
1. Where did Peter go with his sister on Saturday morning?	(5 seconds)	(10 seconds)
2. Why did Cindy go to Rome last weekend?	(5 seconds)	(10 seconds)
3. Why couldn't Cindy's mother come with them?	(5 seconds)	(10 seconds)
4. After Cindy had dinner, what did she do before going to sleep?	(5 seconds)	(10 seconds)

B. Look at the example and practice with a partner. Use the words below or invent your own. (Then change roles and practice again.)

go to the beach / ?
No ⇨ go for a bicycle ride

Did you go to the beach on the weekend?

No, I didn't. I went for a bicycle ride.

go to the Spanish class / ?
No ⇨ watch a comedy show on TV

paint the house / ?
No ⇨ go white-water rafting

The Past Tense

Grammar Focus 1

● Affirmative / Negatives

- To make the simple past of regular verbs, we have to add *-ed* to the base form of the verb. The past form is the same for all the persons. To make the negative of the simple past, we put the helping verb *did* and *not* before base verbs.

They didn't visit Rome.
They visited Athens.

Jessica didn't play tennis yesterday.
She played soccer with some friends.

● Yes/No Questions

- To make a yes/no question, we put *Did* before the subject. We often use *did* in short answers to questions.

Q: Did you learn scuba diving yesterday?
A: Yes, I did.

Q: Did you enjoy the party, Ellen?
A: No, I didn't. I didn't like the food.

Grammar Focus 2

● Irregular Verbs

- Some verbs do not have *-ed* forms. They need special forms in the past tense. Their past forms are irregular.

Base form		Past form		Base form		Past form		Base form		Past form
hear	⇨	heard		sleep	⇨	slept		buy	⇨	bought
sit	⇨	sat		teach	⇨	taught		see	⇨	saw
meet	⇨	met		ride	⇨	rode		go	⇨	went
speak	⇨	spoke		leave	⇨	left		make	⇨	made
take	⇨	took		fly	⇨	flew		give	⇨	gave
drink	⇨	drank		find	⇨	found		have	⇨	had
stand	⇨	stood		wear	⇨	wore		come	⇨	came
write	⇨	wrote		lose	⇨	lost		eat	⇨	ate

17

A. Make yes/no questions and answer.

1. She practiced the piano.   Q: _Did she practice the piano?_   A: No, _she didn't_ .

2. He enjoyed his vacation.   Q: _____   A: Yes, _____ .

3. They liked the film.   Q: _____   A: No, _____ .

4. It rained all day.   Q: _____   A: Yes, _____ .

5. I watched the discussion.   Q: _____   A: No, _____ .

B. Complete the sentences with the simple past of the verbs in brackets.

1. Joe and Sunny _____ _went_ _____ (go) to the beach last Saturday.

2. I _____ (buy) books at the bookstore.

3. She _____ (drink) a cup of coffee this morning.

4. They _____ (wear) bathing suits.

Super Speaking

● Look at the example and practice with a partner. Use the words below or invent your own. (Then change roles and practice again.)

Kevin / study for a test yesterday afternoon
No ⇨ go to the beach

Kevin studied for a test yesterday afternoon.

No, he didn't study for a test.
He went to the beach.

Ava / clean the house on Saturday night
No ⇨ go to the movie theater

Ann and Bob / watch a DVD yesterday
No ⇨ visit their grandparents

Describing People

Building Vocabulary

A. Choose and fill in the blanks to make sentences.

similar	V-neck sweater	blue	long blond
long brown	intelligent	striped T-shirt	thumb

1.

Do you know that girl with
_____long blond_____ hair?

2.

She has _____
eyes.

3.

The boy is wearing a
_____ .

4.

The new secretary has
_____ hair?

5.

My mother is wearing a
_____ .

6.

The girl is _____ and,
what is more, very pretty.

7.

She had one _____ in
her mouth.

8.

Their house is very _____
to ours, but ours is bigger.

B. Read the definitions. Cross out (X) the unnecessary letters and write the correct words.

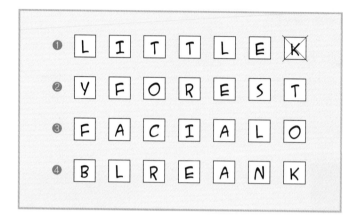

1. small in size ⇨ _little_

2. a large area with many trees ⇨ _____

3. related to the face ⇨ _____

4. to separate into two or more pieces, especially by hitting or dropping something ⇨ _____

C. Read the below sentences and choose the correct answers.

1. People _communicate_ with each other by spoken or written languages or by gestures. In this sentence _communicate_ menas
   (a) to speak or write to someone
   (b) all the people living in one place

2. _Humans_ live in almost every part of the world. In this sentence _Humans_ means
   (a) wanting or needing to eat
   (b) a man, woman, or child; not an animal

3. We believe that the mammoth is the _ancestor_ of modern-day elephants. In this sentence _ancestor_ means
   (a) someone in your family who lived a long time before you were born
   (b) to tell something to a lot of people

A. Read the descriptions and write the names in the boxes.

Harry Potter

Ron Weasley

Hermione Granger

Dumbledore

Profeeor Snape

1. I'm Harry's best friend. I have red hair. I don't like spiders. Who am I?

2. I'm a famous wizard. I'm the headmaster of Hogwart's school. I'm very old. Who am I?

3. My friends are Ron and Hermione. Voldemort killed my parents. I have a scar on my head and I wear glasses. Who am I?

4. I'm very intelligent, but a bit bossy. I have long blond hair and Harry thinks I am quite pretty. Who am I?

5. I'm a professor at Hogwart's school. I'm the head of Slytherin House. I have got black hair and a long nose. I'm evil. Who am I?

B. Fill in the blanks. Then match the questions and responses.

1. ___Is___ Peter young? ___e___   a. Yes, she is. She's really pretty.

2. What _____ your brothers look like? _____   b. No, she doesn't. She has short hair.

3. Do your parents _____ blue eyes? _____   c. She's slim. She has blond curly hair.

4. _____ your sister beautiful? _____   d. I have short hair and blue eyes.

5. What _____ your friend Jane look like? _____   e. No, he isn't. He's 30!

6. _____ your grandparents weak? _____   f. No, they don't. They have black eyes.

7. What _____ you look like? _____   g. They're young and have brown hair.

8. _____ your girlfriend have long hair? _____   h. No, they're not. They're strong.

Super Writing 1

A. Look at the example. Make conversations as in the example.

1.

| a white shirt | | long brown hair |

A: I'm looking for Cindy.

B: Oh, she's wearing a white shirt   .

A: Does she have short hair?

B: No, she has long brown hair   .

2.

| a yellow striped shirt | | long straight black hair |

A: I'm looking for Jessica.

B: Oh, _____ .

A: Does she have reddish-blond hair?

B: No, _____ .

3.

| a white blouse | | black eyes |

A: I'm looking for Lisa.

B: Oh, _____ .

A: Does she have blue eyes?

B: No, _____ .

B. Read and write answers as in the example.

1.

short black hair / blue shirt

Q: Who is Sunny's uncle?

A: He is the man with short black hair   .

　　He is the man in the blue shirt   .

2.

curly brown hair / red sweater

Q: Who is Nancy's aunt?

A: She is the woman with _____ .

　　She is the woman in the _____ .

3.

long straight hair / checkered shirt

Q: Who is Olivia's sister?

A: She is the woman with _____ .

　　She is the woman in the _____ .

- 1~3 Unscramble the words to make sentences.
- 4~7 Sentence Transformation. / S(Statement) / N(Negative) / Q(Question) / T(Tense)

1.

| she | . | and blue eyes | long blond hair | has |

⇨ _____

2.

| a green T-shirt | . | wearing | she | is |

⇨ _____

3.

| are | to | humans | Chimpanzees | . | related | closely |

⇨ _____

4.

You mustn't exercise regularly. (S)

⇨ _____

5.

He is talking to the girl wearing a pair of glasses. (Q)

⇨ _____

6.

They use stones to break hard nuts. (T - Past)

⇨ _____

7.

She is cute and has curly brown hair. (N)

⇨ _____

Super Speaking!

A. Listen to the conversation between two people. Then answer the questions. While you listen, you can take notes. ⊙ Track 25

Listening Notes

	Prepare ●●●	Speak ●●●
1. How often does the woman exercise in a week?	(5 seconds)	(10 seconds)
2. Does Jessica's friend have blond hair?	(5 seconds)	(10 seconds)
3. What are Sunny doing in health club now?	(5 seconds)	(10 seconds)
4. What does Sunny's boss look like?	(5 seconds)	(10 seconds)

B. Choose of the girls(A-D) and describe her. Your partner will guess who she is.

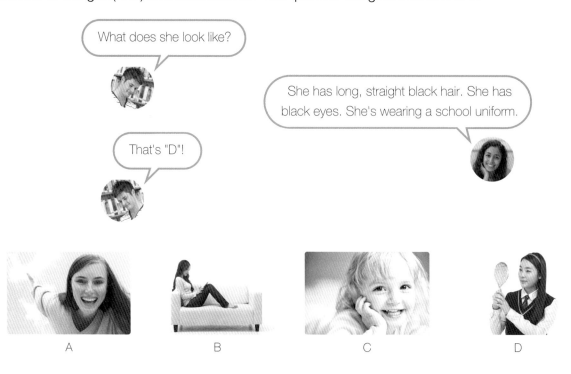

What does she look like?

She has long, straight black hair. She has black eyes. She's wearing a school uniform.

That's "D"!

A   B   C   D

24

Questions with Wh-words

Grammar Focus

● **Information Questions with the Verb Be**

- An information question begins with a question word. In questions with *be*, we put the subject after *be*. The verb *be* tells the tense of the question.

- We use *why* to ask about the reason for something. We use *when* to ask about times and dates. We use *where* to ask about places. We use *who* to ask questions about people. We use *how* to ask about people's health or happiness.

Q: Who is that woman?
A: She's my teacher.

Q: Why is she angry?
A: I don't know!

Q: Where were you yesterday?
A: We were at the library.

Q: What is it?
A: It is a lemon.

Q: When is Valentine's Day?
A: It's on February 14th.

Q: How is she?
A: She is tired.

＊ We use 'What is he(she)?' to ask a question about his/her job.
What is he? - She is a police officer.

A. Make questions with Write *what*, *where*, or *who*. Then circle the correct verb.

1.

Q: _____ are they?

A: They (is / are) books.

2.

Q: _____ is Karen?

A: She (is / are) at the park.

3.

Q: _____ is the woman?

A: She (is / are) my mother.

B. Make questions with *what, who, when, why, how* or *where.*

1.

Q: ___What is he___ ?
A: He is a firefighter.

2.

Q: _____ ?
A: They are at home.

3.

Q: _____ ?
A: They are happy.

4.

Q: _____ ?
A: My birthday is on May 10th.

5.

Q: _____ ?
A: She's taking a taxi because her car isn't working.

6.

Q: _____ ?
A: She's my girlfriend.

Super Speaking

● Look at the example and practice with a partner. Use the words below or invent your own. (Then change roles and practice again.)

when / New Year's Day / ?
⇨ it / on January 1st

When is New Year's Day?

It's on January 1st.

when / Christmas / ?
⇨ it / on December 25th

when / Halloween / ?
⇨ it / on October 31st

what / your favorite sports / ?
⇨ my favorite sports / tennis

Building Vocabulary

A. Look and check the correct words.

1.

playing volleyball _____

playing tennis _____

2.

snowboarding _____

swimming _____

3.

listening _____

singing _____

4.

cooking _____

painting _____

5.

inline skating _____

skateboarding _____

6.

cycling _____

scuba diving _____

7.

musician _____

baker _____

8.

skiing _____

hiking _____

B. Circle the correct words and fill in the blanks.

1.

Collecting old coins is a popular _____.

(hobby / clothes)

2.

When I have spare time, I usually _____.

(ride a horse / surf the Internet)

3.

Tiffany often _____ in the afternoon.

(go shopping / go fishing)

C. Match the words and meanings. Draw a line between the word and its meaning.

WORD

MEANING

1.

paint

a. a type of football game played by two teams of 15 players each

2.

surf the Internet

b. to create a picture or work of art

3.

rugby

c. one's menas of making a living; job

4.

occupation

d. to search from place to place on the Internet for interesting information

D. Read the below sentences and choose the correct answers.

1. He is so *boring*; he never says anything interesting but talks a lot. In this sentence *boring* means
(a) not interesting
(b) very exciting

2. His *reason* for going back to school is to learn new things. In this sentence *reason* means
(a) the purpose for doing
(b) the ability to understand and think logically

A. What is your favorite hobby? Write sentences as in the example.

1.

⇨ _My favorite hobby is reading books._

2.

⇨ _____

3.

⇨ _____

4.

⇨ _____

B. Read and complete the sentences. Then practice with your partner.

1.

watch movies

Q: What do you usually do in your spare time?

A: _When I have free time, I really enjoy watching movies._

2.

go ice skating

Q: What do you usually do in your spare time?

A: _____

3.

go fishing

Q: What do you usually do in your spare time?

A: _____

Super Writing 1

A. Look at the example. Make conversations as in the example.

1.

ice skating / Susan / Saturday	visit my grandmother

A: I'm _going to go ice skating with Susan this Saturday_ .

   Will you join us?

B: I'm sorry, but I can't. I _have to visit my grandmother_ .

2.

buy new clothes / Patricia / Sunday	finish my English class report

A: I'm _____ .

   Will you join us?

B: I'm sorry, but I can't. I _____ .

3.

bowling / George / Thursday	attend a seminar

A: I'm going to _____ .

   Will you join us?

B: I'm sorry, but I can't. I _____ .

B. Look at the example. Write sentences in the same way

1.

(go inline skating / play badminton / my sister or friend)

⇨ In the summer I spend a lot of time outdoors. When it is
sunny I like going inline skating. I also like playing badminton
with my sister or friend.

2.

(go swimming / watch a movie on TV / my father)

⇨ _____

_____

_____ .

3.

(ride my bicycle / listen to K-pop music / my friends)

⇨ _____

_____

_____ .

● 1~3 Unscramble the words to make sentences.
● 4~7 Sentence Transformation. / N(Negative) / Q(Question) / T(Tense)

1.

| I'm | . | football or rugby | good at | not |

⇨ _____

2.

| singing | really | good at | . | that | I'm | she says that |

⇨ _____

3.

| a professional surfer | . | I | to be | in the future | want |

⇨ _____

4.

Reading books helps me to gather much knowledge. (T - Past)

⇨ _____

5.

She has a pair of inline skates at home. (Q)

⇨ _____

6.

Karen likes to sing in front of other people. (N)

⇨ _____

7.

We like travel around the country. (T - Future / be going to)

⇨ _____

Super Speaking!

A. Listen to the conversation between two people. Then answer the questions. While you listen, you can take notes. ⦿ Track 35

Listening Notes

	Prepare ●••	Speak ●••
1. What is William's favorite animation cartoon?	(5 seconds)	(10 seconds)
2. Why does he like the character?	(5 seconds)	(10 seconds)
3. Has Alice ever tried inline skating?	(5 seconds)	(10 seconds)
4. Where are they going to do this Saturday?	(5 seconds)	(10 seconds)
5. Where are they going to meet at ten?	(5 seconds)	(10 seconds)

B. Read and repeat the dialog. Then use the speaking cards to practice it with your partner.

A: Jessica always ❶ __plays games on her computer__ .
B: I don't like ❷ __playing computer games__ .
A: Then what are your hobbies?
B: My hobbies are ❸ __reading__ and ❹ __drawing__ .

❶ goes inline skating on Saturdays
❷ going inline skating
❸ plying the guitar
❹ hanging out with my friends

❶ goes bowling every Sunday
❷ going bowling
❸ playing badminton
❹ watching movies

Verb + Infinitive

Grammar Focus 1

● **Infinitive as Object**

- We use an infinitive (to + the base form of a verb) as the object of certain verbs and constructions. Here are some of the verbs.

We decided to go Hawaii.

The guard refused to let them enter the building.

agree	need
expect	refuse
manage	can't wait
appear	promise
hope	would like
decide	plan
manage	offer

Grammar Focus 2

● **Verb + Gerund or Infinitive**

- Some verbs can take either an infinitive or a gerund. With some verbs, there is no difference in meaning. Here are some examples.

Bob can't stand waiting in long line.
= Bob can't stand to wait in long line.

like	hate	can't stand	continue
love	begin	start	intend

A. Complete the sentences with a gerund and an infinitive of each of the verbs given.

1. **sing** The girl began ___to sing___ .
   The girl began ___singing___ .

2. **do** Steve hates _____ his homework.
   Steve hates _____ his homework.

2. **fight** They started _____ .
   They started _____ .

4. **fly** Does she love _____ kites?
   Does she love _____ kites?

B. Look at the pictures and make sentences using the prompts as in the example. Use an infinitive as the object.

1.

would / you like / drink orange juice / ?

⇨ <u>Would you like to drink orange juice?</u>

2.

Nancy / wants / become a photographer

⇨ _____

3.

you hope / travel by train / ? / do

⇨ _____

4.

Kevin / promised / not / bother her again

⇨ _____

Super Speaking

• Look at the example and practice with a partner. Use the words below or invent your own. (Then change roles and practice again.)

friendly
⇨ swim / read books

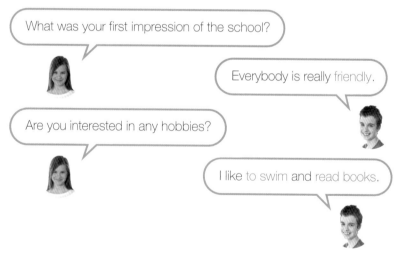

What was your first impression of the school?

Everybody is really friendly.

Are you interested in any hobbies?

I like to swim and read books.

nice
⇨ sing songs / listen to music

fun
⇨ travel / do meditation

attractive
⇨ go scuba diving / shopping

Building Vocabulary

A. Choose and fill in the blanks to make sentences.

science fiction	teenagers	sell	writer
horror movies	publishers	hero	translate

1.

I really don't like _____.

2.

As a matter of fact, I like _____ films.

3.

He is a very popular _____ but I don't like his style.

4.

Many _____ keep in touch with their friends online.

5.

Are you able to _____ English into Korean?

6.

My book was turned down by eight _____.

7.

Today people buy and _____ the things on the Internet.

8.

Who is going to play to the _____ of the play?

B. Match the words and meanings. Draw a line between the word and its meaning.

WORD

MEANING

1.

romance

a. the man to whom a woman is married

2.

character

b. a person or animal who has finished growing physically and mentally

3.

adult

c. a relationship between two people who love each other

4.

husband

d. what a person or thing is like

C. Read the below sentences and choose the correct answers.

1. Are you willing to *donate* your organs after you are dead? In this sentence *donate* means
   (a) to give something to a person or organization that needs help
   (b) in one country and not involving other countries

2. He left a large *fortune* to his two daughters. In this sentence *fortune* means
   (a) happening because of good luck
   (b) a very large amount of money

Super Exercise

A. Complete the conversations. Choose (a), (b) or (c).

What's your favorite movie?

(a) I've never seen it, but I'd like to.
(b) My favorite movie is *Spiderman*.
(c) I like adventure movies. How about you?

1. Do you prefer to watch movies on DVD or in a movie theater?

  (a) Really? Watching horror films helps me relieve stress.

  (b) Do you know the main story of the movie?

  (c) I prefer watching movies in a movie theater. I like the big screen, and sound is fantastic.

2. Have you ever seen the movie *Toy Story*?

  (a) Of course. I like all kind of Disney animation.

  (b) I really like action movies.

  (c) I saw the movie *Finding Nemo*. It's very interesting.

B. What is your favorite movie? Write sentences as in the example.

1.

thriller

⇨ My favorite type of movie is thriller.

2.

horror and comedy

⇨ _____

3.

romance

⇨ _____

4.

science fiction and adventure

⇨ _____

Super Writing 1

A. Look at the example. Make conversations as in the example.

1.

| different cultures / languages | horror movies |

A: I like movies from different countries.

B: What do you like about them?

A: _Well, I can learn about different cultures and languages._
What kind of movies do you usually see?

B: _I like horror movies._

2.

| cultures / languages | action movies |

A: I like movies from different countries.

B: What do you like about them?

A: _____
What kind of movies do you usually see?

B: _____

3.

| cultures / life styles | romantic movies |

A: I like movies from different countries.

B: What do you like about them?

A: _____
What kind of movies do you usually see?

B: _____

B. Look at the example. Write a sentence in the same way.

1.

| Spiderman | special effect / interesting |

⇨ _My favorite movie is Spiderman. It has great special effect and_
the story is interesting.

2.

| Matrix | graphic quality / exciting |

⇨ _____
_____

● 1~3 Unscramble the words to make sentences.
● 4~7 Sentence Transformation. / S(Statement) / N(Negative) / Q(Question) / T(Tense)

1.

| writer | . | a | J.K Rowling | very famous | is |

⇨ _____

2.

| to write the stories | . | a coffee shop | she | to | went |

⇨ _____

3.

| Harry Potter books | for both children and adults | . | very popular |

| became |

⇨ _____

4.

Do you like a musical film? (T - Past)

⇨ _____

5.

Has Jessica traveled by train? (S)

⇨ _____

6.

Hollywood movies are responsible for the behavior of today's youth. (Q)

⇨ _____

7.

I saw the movie Finding Nemo. (N)

⇨ _____

Super Speaking!

A. Listen to the conversation among the people. Then answer the questions. While you listen, you can take notes. (⊙ Track **44**)

Listening Notes

	Prepare ●●●	Speak ●●●
1. Who is the woman?	(5 seconds)	(10 seconds)
2. How often do they go to the movies?	(5 seconds)	(10 seconds)
3. Does Edward like science fiction movies?	(5 seconds)	(10 seconds)
4. What does the woman give to Carol and Edward?	(5 seconds)	(10 seconds)

B. Read and repeat the dialog. Then use the speaking cards to practice it with your partner.

A: Do you go to the movies with your friends?
B: Yes, I do. I go ❶ ___every Saturday___.
A: What kind of movies do you watch?
B: I watch all kinds of movies but ❷ ___science fiction___ movies are my favorite! They're so ❸ ___interesting___ and ❹ ___exciting___!

❶ every Sunday
❷ action
❸ exciting
❹ thrilling

❶ every Friday
❷ animated
❸ cute
❹ vivid

Grammar Focus 1

● **The Present Perfect: meaning**

- We use the present perfect(*have/has* + past participle) for an action or situation that happened in the recent past, without saying an exact time. We also use them with a repeated activity before now.

Shirley and Frank have already had lunch.

Shirley has visited Korea many times.

She has eaten Korean food.

Grammar Focus 2

● **The Present Perfect: for and since**

- We often use the present perfect with *for* and *since*. We use *for* and *since* with the present perfect to say how long the action or situation lasted from the past to the present.

A: How long have you lived in Miami?

B: I have lived here for six months.

C: I have lived here since last year. I'm really happy here.

A. Complete the questions and the answers. Use the verbs in brackets.

1. Q: _____Have_____ you _____eaten_____ (eat) the pizza?   A: No, I ____haven't____ .

2. Q: _____ Joseph _____ (lose) his basketball?   A: Yes, he _____ .

3. Q: _____ we _____ (have) an email from them?   A: Yes, we _____ .

4. Q: _____ Gregory and Megan _____ (see) the movie?   A: No, they _____ .

5. Q: _____ Mom and you _____ (call) Grandma to say thank you?
A: Yes, we _____ .

B. Look at the pictures and the prompts. Write sentences as in the example. Use the present perfect with *for* or *since*.

1.

Kathy is a teacher.

she / teach / English / five years

⇨ *She has taught English for five years.*

2.

Donald's hobby is collecting stamps.

he / collect / stamps / 2004

⇨ _____

3.

Alex and Sarah work for the company.

they / work / for the company / ten years

⇨ _____

4.

It rains everywhere.

it / rain / everywhere / last night

⇨ _____

Super Speaking

● Look at the example and practice with a partner. Use the words below or invent your own. (Then change roles and practice again.)

you / love / Cindy / ?
⇨ since the day I met her

How long have you loved Cindy?

I have loved her since the day I met her.

Jessica / study / English / ?
⇨ for three years

you / live / in this country / ?
⇨ since last year

Billy / be looking for / a job / ?
⇨ for ten months

Building Vocabulary

A. Look and check the correct words.

1.
Joseph

cold and snowy _____

warm and cloud _____

2.
Karen

windy and rainy _____

warm and sunny _____

3.
Albert

cool and cloudy _____

hot and humid _____

4.
Jessica

windy and rainy _____

cool and windy _____

B. Practice the conversation with your partner using the words above.

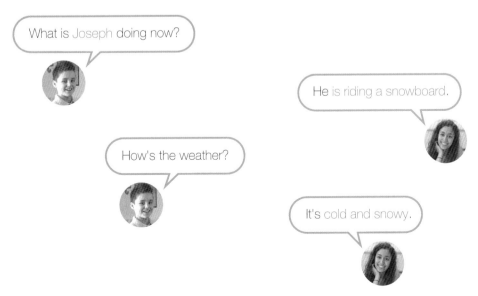

What is Joseph doing now?

He is riding a snowboard.

How's the weather?

It's cold and snowy.

C. Choose and fill in the blanks to make sentences.

> thunderstorm   brightly   autumn   numerous

1.

_____ tinges the woods with a thousand beautiful varieties of color.

2.

The moon was shining _____.

3.

_____ people attended the rock concert.

4.

Lightning often occurs during a _____.

D. Read the below sentences and choose the correct answers.

1. It was a *relief* to know that she was safe. In this sentence *relief* means
   (a) a feeling of happiness because something bad did not happen or is finished
   (b) belief in one or more gods

2. Don't worry about it. Just try to *relax*. In this sentence *relax* menas
   (a) to decide that you do not want something or someone
   (b) to become less worried or angry and more calm

3. She likes to wear expensive *clothes*. In this sentence *clothes* menas
   (a) things that you wear on your body
   (b) a person who wears funny clothes and tries to make people laugh

4. The *temperature* outside is chilly today. In this sentence *temperature* menas
   (a) the way you feel, especially when you are angry
   (b) the degree of heat or cold

A. Read the following passage. Then choose the best answers to each question.

In England, people often talk about the weather because they can experience four seasons in one day. In the morning the weather is warm just like in spring. An hour later, black clouds come and then it rains hard. The weather gets a little cold. In the late afternoon, the sky will be sunny, the sun will begin to shine, and it will be summer at this time of a day. In England, people can also have summer in winter, or have winter in summer. So in winter they can swim sometimes, and in summer sometimes they should take warm clothes. When you go to England, you will see that some English people usually take an umbrella or a raincoat with them in the sunny morning, but you should not laugh at them. If you don't take an umbrella or a raincoat, you will regret later in the day.

1. Why do people in England often talk about the weather?

(a) Because they may have four seasons in one day

(b) Because they often have very good weather

(c) Because the weather is warm just like in spring

(d) Because the sky is sunny all day

2. From the story we know that when _____ come, there is a heavy rain.

(a) sunshine and snow   (b) black clouds

(c) summer and winter   (d) spring and autumn

3. "People can also have summer in winter." means "It is sometimes too _____ in winter."

(a) warm   (b) cool   (c) cold   (d) rainy

4. In the sunny morning some English people usually take a raincoat or an umbrella with them because

_____.

(a) their friends ask them to do so   (b) it often rains in England

(c) they are going to sell them   (d) they are their favorite things

5. The best title for this passage is _____.

(a) Bad Seasons   (b) Summer or Winter

(c) The Weather in England   (d) Strange English People

Super Writing 1

A. Look at the example. Make conversations as in the example.

1.

Alaska / cold and snowy	take a coat

A: I'm going to go to Alaska.
B: How is the weather there?
A: It's cold and snowy.
B: I think you should take a coat.

2.

Cairo / hot and dry	pack sunglasses

A: _____
B: How is the weather there?
A: _____
B: _____

3.

London / windy and cold	take a muffler and gloves

A: _____
B: How is the weather there?
A: _____
B: _____

B. Look at the example. Write sentences in the same way.

1.

spring / boat / pleasant and refreshing

⇨ My favorite season is spring because I love to go boating.
   In spring, weather is pleasant and refreshing.

2.

summer / camp / warm and the sun shines throughout the day

⇨ _____
   _____

3.

winter / ski or snowboard / mostly cold and snowy

⇨ _____
   _____

● 1~3 Unscramble the words to make sentences.
● 4~7 Sentence Transformation. / S(Statement) / Q(Question) / T(Tense)

1.

the four seasons of the year . are spring, summer, autumn, and winter

⇨ _____

2.

wake up early . don't have to I and go to school

⇨ _____

3.

of the year summer . is the hottest season

⇨ _____

4.

There was a lot of rain and strong winds. (Q)

⇨ _____

5.

Do your moods change with weather? (S / T - Past)

⇨ _____

6.

Many icebergs were melting because of global warming. (T - Present)

⇨ _____

7.

A cheetah is the fastest animal in the world. (Q)

⇨ _____

Super Speaking!

A. Read and repeat the dialog. Then use the speaking cards to practice it with your partner.

A: Hello.

B: Hi, _____Emma_____. Where are you?

A: We are on holiday in _____Italy_____.

B: What's the weather like?

A: _____It's sunny_____.

B: What are you doing at the moment?

A: We're _____having lunch_____.

Emma and Robin
Italy
have lunch

Sue and David
London
sit in a cafe

Ron and his brother
Scotland
play computer games

B. Look at the example and practice with a partner. Use the words below or invent your own. (Then change roles and practice again.)

Seattle / ?
⇨ sunny and hot / a skirt

What's the weather like in Seattle?

It's sunny and hot.

What are you wearing now?

I'm wearing a skirt.

Seoul / ?
⇨ windy and cold / a sweater

Beijing / ?
⇨ warm and windy /
   a white shirt and blue jeans

London / ?
⇨ warm and cloudy /
   a school uniform

Superlative

Grammar Focus

● **Superlative Form: -est and most**

- We use *the* + the superlative form to compare three or more people or things. We use the definite article *the* before superlative adjectives and adverbs.

- After superlatives, we use *in* with places (towns, buildings etc.). We also use *in* for organizations and groups of people (class, team, company etc.).

- After superlatives, we often use *of* before expressions of time and quantity, and plural nouns.

What is the longest river in the world? (not 'of the world')

Yesterday was the hottest day of the year. (not 'in the year')

The snail moves the most slowly of all animals. (not 'in all animals')

Jessica is the most active student in class. (not 'of class')

A. Complete the sentences with the superlative form of the words in brackets.

1. The Eiffel Tower in Paris is _____*the most famous*_____ (famous) building in France.

2. Australia is _____ (small) continent, but it's a very large country.

3. The Taj Mahal is _____ (beautiful) building in the world.

4. The Nile is _____ (long) river in the world.

5. Peter can run _____ (fast) of them all.

B. Look at the pictures. Write sentences with superlatives of the words in brackets.

1.  2.  3. 4.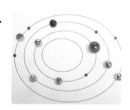

1. The blue whale is the biggest of all animals.

(the blue whale / of all animals / big)

2. _____

(the giraffe / in the world / tall animal)

3. _____

(the ostrich / in the world / big bird

4. _____

(the Pluto / from the sun / far planet)

Super Speaking

● Look at the example and practice with a partner. Ask and answer questions about your country. Give complete answers.

Which is the biggest city in Korea?

Seoul is the biggest city in Korea.

Your turn to ask now!

1. the biggest city	2. the largest airport	3. the tallest building
4. the busiest street	5. the coldest month	6. the hottest month
7. the oldest building	8. the longest river	9. the highest mountain
10. the most crowded city	11. the farthest city	12. the most famous church

Summer Plans

Building Vocabulary

A. Choose and fill in the blanks to make sentences.

during	forget	housework	Dokdo
cabin	campfire	nature	the Stature of Liberty

1.

South Korea calls the islands

_____ .

2.

In 1884, France presented _____
to America.

3.

Do you usually help your wife a lot with
the _____ ?

4.

I'd like to go hanggliding _____
our summer break.

5.

The _____ in the
countryside is very beautiful.

6.

Don't _____ to fasten your
seatbelt.

7.

There is a _____ in a clearing
in the forest.

8.

People are playing around a
_____ .

B. Match the words and meanings. Draw a line between the word and its meaning.

1.

countryside

2.

canoe

3.

university

4.

company

a. a light, narrow type of boat

b. the land outside a city or town with trees, farms, and few houses

c. a group of people doing business

d. a college or collection of colleges at which people study for a degree

C. Read the below sentences and choose the correct answer.

1. It is adventurous and *exciting* seeing the world. In this sentence *exciting* means

(a) making you feel excited

(b) feeling unhappy, especially because something bad has happened

2. A birthday party is a *special* occasion. In this sentence *special* means

(a) not kknow about by other people

(b) different from and usually better than what is normal or ordinary

A. Complete the conversations. Choose (a), (b) or (c).

Are you going anywhere for the summer?

(a) I'm taking off for Seattle next week.
(b) Yes, I'm going to Hawaii.
(c) Yes, I intend to finish this work by tomorrow.

1. So, Steve, do you have anything planned for the weekend?

(a) Not really. But I'm going to the movies tonight.

(b) Oh, who with?

(c) We often go hiking in the summer. Maybe twice a month.

2. What are they doing in June?

(a) I'm taking a scuba diving course.

(b) He's looking for the school festival.

(c) They're taking a trip to the mountains.

B. What are you doing this summer? Write sentences as in the example.

1.

go camping / with my family

⇨ I'm going camping with my family.

2.

travel / with my girlfriend

⇨ _____

3.

spend time / with my friends

⇨ _____

4.

go to the beach

⇨ _____

53

Super Writing 1

A. Look at the example. Make conversations as in the example.

1.

| this weekend | babysit my baby |

A: *What are you doing this weekend?*
B: *I'm babysitting my baby.*

2.

| next week | leave my old apartment and I'm throwing a moving party |

A: _____
B: _____

3.

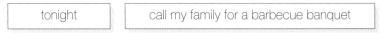

| tonight | call my family for a barbecue banquet |

A: _____
B: _____

4.

| next Saturday | go to the beach with my family |

A: _____
B: _____

B. Look at the pictures. Write sentences using the phrases in the box.

at the beach / three days   in the woods / five days   at the farm / two weeks

1.

We stayed in the woods for
five days.

2.

_____

_____

3.

_____

_____

● 1~3 Unscramble the words to make sentences.
● 4~7 Sentence Transformation. / Q(Question) / T(Tense)

1.

to Haeundae　.　promised　my dad　to go

⇨ _____

2.

with housework　to help　.　my mother　I'm going

⇨ _____

3.

for this summer　any special plans　?　do you have

⇨ _____

4.

are you going　who　?　to travel with

⇨ _____

5.

Schools, temples, or churches have special programs for this summer. (Q)

⇨ _____

6.

I visit Namsan hanok village. (T - Future / be going to)

⇨ _____

7.

The children stay there for four weeks and sleep in tents or cabins. (T - Past)

⇨ _____

Super Speaking!

A. Draw lines to match the places to the activities. Choose an activity and then have a conversation with your partner.

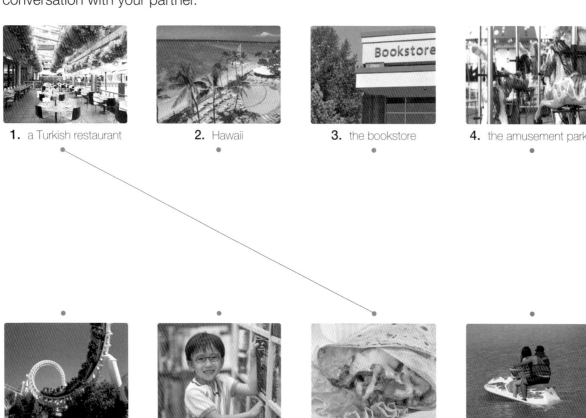

1. a Turkish restaurant   **2.** Hawaii   **3.** the bookstore   **4.** the amusement park

a. ride a rollercoaster   b. buy some English books   c. eat a kebab   d. ride a jet ski

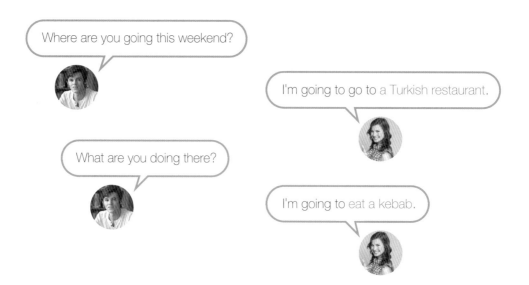

Where are you going this weekend?

I'm going to go to a Turkish restaurant.

What are you doing there?

I'm going to eat a kebab.

The Present Progressive as a Future Tense / Participles as Adjectives

Grammar Focus 1

● **Future: present progressive**

- We use *be going to* for plans and intentions for the (near) future.

- We use present progressive to talk about future plans. We use the present progressive especially with verbs of movement and transport such as *come*, *go*, *fly*, *travel* and *leave*. The present progressive for the future and *be going to* have similar meanings.

He is having a meeting with his boss in an hour. (He has already arranged it.)

We're taking a trip to Hawaii next year. (We have already arranged it.)

Grammar Focus 2

● **Participles as Adjectives**

- We can use present participles and past participles of verbs as adjectives.

- Present participles used as adjectives describe the person or things that produces the feeling.

- Past participles used as adjectives describe how people feel about something or someone.

The past participle made by adding -ed to the verb, e.g. walk ⇨ walked

This movie is boring. Let's stop watching it.

The present participle made by adding -ing to the verb, e.g. walk ⇨ walking

I'm bored of my job. I want to find another one.

A. Complete the sentences. Use the simple progressive.

1. Q: What is Bob doing this Saturday?

A: He is reading a book.   . (read / a book)

2. Q: What are Jane and Tom doing tonight?

A: _____. (go / to the movie theater)

3. Q: What is Isabella doing this Sunday?

A: _____. (play tennis / with her father)

B. Read and circle the correct words.

1. This was a very (fascinating / fascinated) book.

2. At first I thought it was (boring / bored), but it wasn't.

3. We were (shocked / shocking) to know it was based on a true story.

4. I read the book quickly because it was so (interested / interesting).

Super Speaking

● Look at the example and practice with a partner. Use the words below or invent your own. (Then change roles and practice again.)

take a drive to the beach

study chemistry

I'm taking a drive to the beach this weekend. What are you doing this weekend?

I'm studying chemistry.

go bungee jumping

visit Seoul with a friend

take swimming lessons

meet my boyfriend

spend time with my friends

go shopping with my mother

stay home

visit my grandmother

Building Vocabulary

A. Look and check the correct words.

1.

drive my car _____
take a bus _____

2.

ride my bicycle _____
walk to school _____

3.

take the trolley _____
take the subway _____

4.

get a ride _____
catch the bus _____

5.

ride my bicycle _____
take the train _____

6.

take a taxi _____
get off at the next stop _____

B. Circle the correct words and fill in the blanks.

1.

Most people who live in cities get around using _____.

(public transportation / the school bus)

2.

Using diet pills is not a _____ way to lose weight.

(harmful / safe)

3.

This is the last _____ for me to go abroad.

(opportunity / familiar)

C. Match the words and meanings. Draw a line between the word and its meaning.

WORD

MEANING

1.

chat

• a. not enjoyable or uncomfortable

2.

quickly

• b. to talk with someone in a friendly way

3.

rush hour

• c. a time when traffic is very heavy, esp. when people are going to and from work

4.

unpleasant

• d. fast or in a short time

D. Read the below sentences and choose the correct answers.

1. In that area the houses stand *close* together. In this sentence *close* means
   (a) near in distance   (b) to shut something

2. We had no *means* of communication. In this sentence *means* means
   (a) to have a particular meaning   (b) a way of doing something

3. The soft and *familiar* voice came in my ear. In this sentence *familiar* means
   (a) well known to you, or easily recognized by you
   (b) a group of people who are related to each other, especially parents and children

A. Complete the conversations. Choose (a), (b) or (c).

How did you get to your uncle's house?

(a) I took an express bus. It was much better than a car.
(b) I get sick easily when I get on a boat.
(c) You should take the train at 7 p.m.

1. How much luggage do you have?

   (a) We will be crossing by ferry.

   (b) I have two suitcases to check in.

   (c) Are you going to take the bus downtown?

2. How are you going to get home from the restaurant on Sunday, Peter?

   (a) A ticket to San Francisco, please.

   (b) They'll get there by airplane.

   (c) Oh, I can just take a bus or a taxi. There are usually plenty of taxis around that area at night.

B. Match questions and answers.

1. How does she get to her aunt's house?   a. No, she doesn't. She takes the subway.

2. How long does it take for him to get to work? b. We will be crossing by ferry.

3. Does Cindy drive to work?   c. She takes the bus.

4. How do we cross the river?   d. There are no tickets available today.

5. Can I get a train ticket to Chicago?   e. It takes about thirty minutes.

Super Writing 1

A. Look at the example. Make conversations as in the example.

1.

| catch a taxi | 20 minutes by taxi |

A: How do you get to school?

B: Well, I usually catch a taxi.

A: How long does it take from home to school?

B: It takes about 20 minutes by taxi.

2.

| take the subway | 10 minutes by subway |

A:

B:

A:

B:

3.

| walk | 15 minutes to walk |

A:

B:

A:

B:

B. How do these people go to work? Look at the pictures and write sentences.

1. 30 min.  Joseph

2. 15 min. 61 Bob

3. 40 min. Jessica

Joseph rides his bike to work every day. It takes about thirty minutes.

62

• 1~3 Unscramble the words to make sentences.
• 4~7 Sentence Transformation. / N(Negative) / Q(Question) / T(Tense)

1.

| every day | . | ride | I | to school | my bicycle |

⇨ _____

2.

| in some cities | The subway | . | widely used | is also |

⇨ _____

3.

| with their friends | . | to chat | It also gives students opportunity |

⇨ _____

4.

| First, you need | to your destination | . | a ticket | to buy |

⇨ _____

5.

I ride my bicycle to the subway station. (T - Past)

⇨ _____

6.

People should stop using fossil fuels for transit and start using renewable energy sources. (Q)

⇨ _____

7.

Shakespeare wrote these books. (N)

⇨ _____

Super Speaking!

A. Look at the example and practice with a partner. Use the words below or invent your own. (Then change roles and practice again.)

20 minutes / school bus

How long does it take you to get to school?

It takes me 20 minutes to go to school by school bus.

30 minutes / by subway

50 minutes / by train

10 minutes / on foot

B. Ask and answer questions about the places in your neighborhood with your partner.

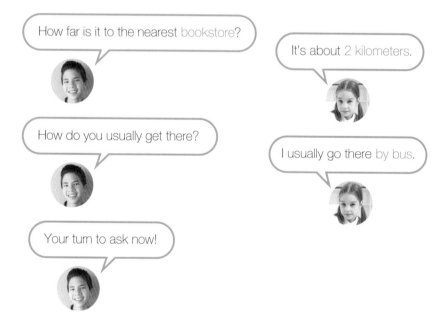

How far is it to the nearest bookstore?

It's about 2 kilometers.

How do you usually get there?

I usually go there by bus.

Your turn to ask now!

bookstore / 2 kilometers
⇨ by bus

hospital / 5 kilometers
⇨ by taxi

museum / 10 kilometers
⇨ by subway

park / 1 kilometer
⇨ by bike

The Passive

Grammar Focus 1

● **Passive: Affirmative (be + V-ed)**

- We use the active form to say what the subject does. We use the passive voice when the result of the action is more important than the person doing the action. The actor(subject) of the verb comes after '*by*'. The object of the active voice sentence becomes the subject of the passive voice sentence.

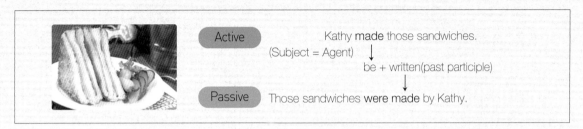

Active   Kathy **made** those sandwiches.
(Subject = Agent)
                  be + written(past participle)
Passive   Those sandwiches **were made** by Kathy.

- We use the passive when we don't know who did something, or who does something is obvious or not important. We don't use the agent(by + actor).

The temple was destroyed in 1999. (We don't know who destroyed it.)

English is spoken all over the world. (by people)

Rice is grown in Korea. (Who grows it isn't important.)

	Subject	Be	Verb+ -ed	by	Object(Agent)
Present / Past Passive	I	am / was	invited	by	them. / her. / Tom.
	He, She, It, Thing	is / was			
	You, We, They, Things	are / were			

A. Write the past form and past participle.

Base form	Past	Be + Past participle
1. speak	*spoke*	be *spoken*
2. write		be
3. paint		be
4. grow		be
5. visit		be
6. steal		be
7. eat		be

B. Look at the pictures and answer the questions as in the example. Include the *by*-phrase only if necessary.

1.

A: What happened in this picture?

B: ___The mails were delivered by the postman.___

(the mails / deliver / the postman)

2.

A: What happened in this picture?

B: _____

(my laptop / steal)

3.

A: What happened in this picture?

B: _____

(the room / clean / My mother)

4.

A: What happened in this picture?

B: _____

(that house / build / in the middle ages)

Super Speaking

● Look at the example and practice with a partner. Ask and answer the following questions using a passive structure.

Who discovered America?

America was discovered by Columbus.

Your turn to ask now!

Who discovered America? (Columbus)   Who wrote *The Origin of Species*? (Darwin)

Who painted *The Sunflowers*? (Van Gogh)   Who composed For *Elisa*? (Beethoven)

Who wrote *Hamlet*? (Shakespeare)   Who painted the *Mona Lisa*? (Leonardo da Vinci)

Who discovered *The Law of Gravity*? (Newton) Who invented the telephone? (Alexander Graham Bell)

Unit 9 Invitations

Building Vocabulary

A. Choose and fill in the blanks to make sentences.

go camping	crowded	Would you like to	bedroom
a meal	soccer match	wedding invitations	sent

1.

_____ come to my party?

2.

After the movie, we went for _____ in a Korean restaurant.

3.

We sent out more than 300 _____.

4.

The subway was very _____, so we had to stand.

5.

If I stay home tomorrow, I will clean my _____.

6.

Korea and Japan had a friendly _____ yesterday.

7.

We _____ Mom flowers for Mother's Day.

8.

You should take a tent along if you _____.

B. Match the words and meanings. Draw a line between the word and its meaning.

WORD

MEANING

1.

finish

a. to ask someone to come to your house, to a party, etc.

2.

meal

b. one of these regular occasions or times for eating food

3.

invite

c. a performance of music, with or without singing

4.

concert

d. to stop doing something because nothing more needs to be done

C. Read the below sentences and choose the correct answers.

1. He had a sad *expression* on his face. In this sentence *expression* means
(a) the look on someone's face showing what they feel or think
(b) to try to find someone or something

2. He's not *real*, you know. He's just a character in a book. In this sentence *real* means
(a) not true or correct
(b) existing and not imagined

Super Exercise

A. Choose and complete the expressions from the box.

> Sorry, I can't   Yes, I'd love to
>
> Would you like to   How about you

1. _____ come to my party on Friday, Sarah?

2. _____. Thanks, Richard!

3. _____, Joseph? Can you come to my party?

3. _____. I have to finish my school project.

B. Translate in your language and number in order.

1. I'm thinking about Thursday. ⇨ _____

2. If you're free, how about lunch together? ⇨ _____

3. That will be fine with me. ⇨ _____

4. When do you think is okay? ⇨ _____

2 ⇨ ☐ ⇨ ☐ ⇨ ☐

Super Writing 1

A. Look at the example. Make conversation as in the example.

1.

| go camping this weekend | have to finish my homework |

A: _Would you like to go camping this weekend?_

B: _I'd really like to. but I have to finish my homework._

2.

| see a movie on Tuesday night | have to ask my mom first |

A: _____

B: _____

3.

| join us for dinner | have a project to do today |

A: _____

B: _____

4.

| go skiing this weekend | am going to a concert |

A: _____

B: _____

B. Why can't these people go out? Look at the pictures and write their excuses as in the example.

baby-sit / on Saturday

do our science project / on Sunday night

practice the cello / an hour every night

1. I'm sorry, _____ I have to baby-sit on Saturday _____.

2. We're sorry, _____.

3. I'm sorry, _____.

● 1~3 Unscramble the words to make sentences.
● 4~7 Sentence Transformation. / N(Negative) / Q(Question) / T(Tense)

1.

| this afternoon | ? | to do | what | are you | doing |

⇨ _____

2.

| . | Sorry, I can't | I | . | my school project | have to finish |

⇨ _____

3.

| I've promised | . | with my sister | to the movie theater | to go |

⇨ _____

4.

| people | for a meal | . | often invite | in Britain, | friends |

⇨ _____

5.

It's Kathy's birthday next week. (Q)

⇨ _____

6.

There are 15 people staying at our house. (T - Past)

⇨ _____

7.

Let's go out for a meal. (N)

⇨ _____

Super Speaking!

A. Look at the example and practice with a partner. Use the words below or invent your own.
(Then change roles and practice again.)

roller-skating / this Saturday afternoon / ?
⇨ Sunday afternoon / ?

 Would you like to go roller-skating with me this Saturday afternoon?

I would really love to, but I can't.

 What about Sunday afternoon?

That would be nice.

1.

to a movie / this Friday afternoon / ?
⇨ Saturday afternoon / ?

2.

bowling / this Saturday night / ?
⇨ Sunday night / ?

3.

shopping / this weekend / ?
⇨ next weekend / ?

4.

camping / Sunday afternoon / ?
⇨ Monday afternoon / ?

Suggestion: Let's / Would you like

Grammar Focus 1

● **Let's**

- We use *let's* + the base verb without *to* when we want to make a suggestion, something that we can do together.

- *Let's* is the contracted form of *let us*, and the meaning is the same as *why don't we*.

- The negative form is *let's not* + base verb.

Let's + Base verb	Let's + Not + Base verb

A: It's a beautiful day today. What should we do? B: Let's go to Seoul Land. A: That sounds great.	A: I'm tired. B: I'm tired, too. Let's not go to the movie theater tonight.

Grammar Focus 2

● **Would You Like**

- To offer some things, we use *Would you like ...?* (not 'do you like')

- To invite someone, we use *Would you like to ...?* (not 'do you like to')

A: Would you like a cup of coffee? B: Yes, please.	A: Would you like to come to dinner tomorrow evening? B: Yes, I'd love to.

A. Read and rewrite the sentences with *Let's*.

1. Why don't we go to the beach. ⇨ *Let's go to the beach.*

2. Why don't we go to a baseball game? ⇨ _____

3. Why don't we leave at six-thirty? ⇨ _____

4. Why don't we eat out for dinner? ⇨ _____

5. Why don't we send Harry an e-mail? ⇨ _____

B. Complete the sentences with *Do you like* or *Would you like*.

1. *Would you like* _____ to go to the movie theater tonight? - Yes, I'd love to.

2. *Do you like* _____ to watch horror movies? - No, I don't. I prefer romantic comedies.

3. _____ a cup of coffee? - Yes, please. With milk and sugar.

4. _____ to learn Korean? Yes, I do. I love learning Korean.

5. _____ to study history? - Yes, I do. It's very interesting.

6. _____ to go to Sydney? - Oh, yes, I'd love to. I want to see the Opera House.

Super Speaking

● Look at the example and practice with a partner. Use the words below or invent your own.
(Then change roles and practice again.)

Sydney / the Opera House

Where would you like to go on vacation?

I'd like to go to Sydney to see the opera house.

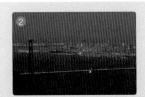

San Francisco / the Golden Gate

London / the Buckingham Place

Scotland / the Loch Ness Monster

Around Town

Building Vocabulary

A. Choose and fill in the blanks to make sentences.

neighborhood	hair salon	amusement park	go straight
dry cleaner's	quiet	cross the street	flower shop

1.

_____ for two blocks and turn right at the post office.

2.

Some people _____.

3.

People are very kind and humorous in my _____.

4.

You should be _____ in the library.

5.

The woman worked at the _____.

6.

I get my hair cut at Eric's _____.

7.

Children are riding a roller coaster at the _____.

8.

Do you know of a _____ nearby?

B. Match the words and meanings. Draw a line between the word and its meaning.

WORD **MEANING**

1.

bookstore

a. a road in a town or city with buildings next to it

2.

street

b. a store that sells medicine

3.

pharmacy

c. a store that sells books

4.

similar

d. almost the same, but not exactly the same

C. Read the below sentences and choose the correct answers.

1. Do you have a *map* of Seoul? In this sentence *map* means
   (a) a drawing of country or an area
   (b) the way in which something is done or happens

2. He is on a business *trip* to New York. In this sentence *trip* means
   (a) something that you do to deceive someone
   (b) an occasion when you go from one place to another

A. Look at the map. Read the sentences and check T(true) or F(false). Rewrite the incorrect sentences.

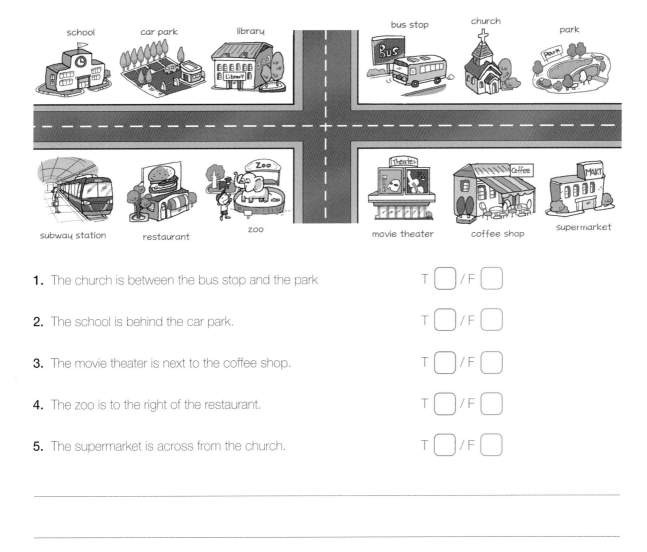

1. The church is between the bus stop and the park   T ◯ / F ◯

2. The school is behind the car park.   T ◯ / F ◯

3. The movie theater is next to the coffee shop.   T ◯ / F ◯

4. The zoo is to the right of the restaurant.   T ◯ / F ◯

5. The supermarket is across from the church.   T ◯ / F ◯

_____

_____

B. Complete the sentences with *There is* or *There are*.

1. _____ an elephant in the zoo.   2. _____ two ponds in the park.

3. _____ two trees next to the library.   4. _____ a man at the subway station.

5. _____ a bus at the bus stop.   6. _____ two flowers next to the school.

Super Writing 1

A. Look at the example. Make conversations as in the example.

1.

(the restaurant on this map)　(two blocks and turn right)　(next to the park)

A: _Excuse me. I'm looking for the restaurant on this map._
Could you help me? How do I get there?
B: _Yes. Go straight for two blocks and turn right. It's next to the park._

2.

(the movie theater on this map)　(one block and turn right)　(next to the bank)

A: _____
Could you help me? How do I get there?
B: _____

3.

(the bookstore on this map)　(two blocks and turn left)　(across from the library)

A: _____
Could you help me? How do I get there?
B: _____

4.

(the bakery on this map)　(one block and turn left)　(in front of the library)

A: _____
Could you help me? How do I get there?
B: _____

5.

(the post office on this map)　(two blocks and turn right)　(next to the school)

A: _____
Could you help me? How do I get there?
B: _____

● 1~4 Unscramble the words to make sentences.
● 5~7 Sentence Transformation. / N(Negative) / Q(Question) / T(Tense)

1.

| have lived | I | for five years | in my perfect neighborhood | . |

⇨ _____

2.

| between | . | my house | a big park and a post office | is |

⇨ _____

3.

| with my dad | . | in the park | on the weekend | sometimes jog | I |

⇨ _____

4.

| to get to school | I | to take two buses | need | . |

⇨ _____

5.

There is a bookstore where students can buy their textbooks. (Q)

⇨ _____

6.

In fact, I need about 10 minutes walk to the bus stop. (T - Past)

⇨ _____

7.

The restaurant is between the shoe shop and the post office. (N)

⇨ _____

Super Speaking!

A. Listen to the dialog again. Please circle the correct words. (•) Track 87

Cindy: Wow, this is [(a) so / (b) such] a big city! Look at the tall buildings!

Brian: Yes, I'm sure you'll love it here, Cindy.

Cindy: Is there any m＿＿＿＿＿＿ t＿＿＿＿＿＿ near here?

Brian: Yes, The movies theater in the city is nearby.

Cindy: That's great. How do I get there?

Brian: Go straight for two b＿＿＿＿＿ and turn [(a) right / (b) left] at the corner. It's on your left.

Cindy: Thanks. [(a) How / (b) What] long will it take?

Brian: It'll take about 20 minutes.

Cindy: Is there a hanok village?

Brian: It's not f＿＿＿＿＿ from here. Go straight for one block. And then turn left at the corner. It's on your right. It's n＿＿＿＿＿ the Hana Middle School.

Cindy: How long will it take?

Brian: It'll only take [(a) for / (b) about] 5 minutes. Last week, I visited the hanok village with my Korean friend, Suji. [(a) When / (b) Where] we arrived at the village, I said, "Wow Did we take a time machine?" Suji said, "Yeah, we're in a＿＿＿＿＿ Korean now." The village was a＿＿＿＿＿ . Every house looked s＿＿＿＿＿ , but each one was [(a) same / (b) different].

B. [Let's Talk] Ask and answer the questions about the dialog with your partner.

1. Is there any movie theater near here?

⇨ Yes, The movies theater ＿＿＿＿＿＿＿＿＿＿＿＿＿＿＿＿＿＿＿＿＿＿＿＿＿＿＿＿＿ .

2. Can you tell me the way to the movie theater?

⇨ Go straight ＿＿＿＿＿＿＿＿＿＿＿＿＿＿＿＿＿＿＿＿＿＿＿＿ . It's on your left.

3. Could you tell me how to get to the hanok village?

⇨ Go straight ＿＿＿＿＿＿＿＿＿ . And then ＿＿＿＿＿＿＿＿＿＿＿＿＿ . It's on your right.

4. How long does it take to get to the hanok village?

⇨ It'll only ＿＿＿＿＿＿＿＿＿＿＿＿＿＿＿＿＿＿＿＿＿＿＿＿＿＿＿＿＿ .

Language Focus! Prepositions of Place

Grammar Focus

● **Prepositions of place**

- We use prepositions of place to talk about where things or people are.

at the door

at the bus stop

at home

on the box

in the box

under the tree

on the horse

next to(=by) the bag

behind the door

in front of the bus

The picture is above the bed.

near the bank

opposite the woman

above the clouds

The house is between the bank and the post office.

The sofa is below the picture.

Kevin's car is parked in front of our house. There's a bus stop opposite our house.

81

A. Answer the questions. Use *in/at/on* + the words below.

1.

the balcony

Q: Where is she standing? A: *On the balcony.*

2.

the bus stop

Q: Where are they? A: _____

3.

the airport

Q: Where is Jane? A: _____

4.

the wall

Q: Where is the clolck? A: _____

5.

the bus

Q: Where are they? A: _____

6.

the table

Q: Where is the woman? A: _____

B. Describe the pictures by completing the sentences with prepositional expressions of place.

1.

The plane flew ___*above*___ the clouds.

2.

Kevin's sitting _____ Olivia.

3.

They are _____ the Eiffel Tower.

4.

The house is _____ the bank _____ the post office.

Building Vocabulary

A. Choose and fill in the blanks to make sentences.

interesting	impressed	taking a photo	grandparents
vacation	airplane	cheap	tourist sight

1.

We had a fantastic time on our _____ in Rome.

2.

They come here to visit her _____ in Korea.

3.

The _____ was flying at an altitude of 30,000 feet.

4.

These shoes are very _____ so I'll get them.

5.

It is Cambodia's biggest _____.

6.

I am extremely _____ by this book.

7.

The woman is _____.

8.

Math is the most _____ subject to me.

B. Match the words and meanings. Draw a line between the word and its meaning.

WORD

MEANING

1.

present

a. a card, often with a picture on the front, that you send in the mail without an envelope

2.

postcard

b. something that happens to you

3.

scary

c. something that you give someone

4.

experience

d. very frightening

C. Read the below sentences and choose the correct answer.

1. When I was young, I thought *adventure* would be boring. In this sentence *adventure* meas

(a) an exciting thing that happens to someone

(b) something that helps you

2. I accepted her *challenge* to a badminton match. In this sentence *challenge* menas

(a) a competition to find who is the best at something

(b) something difficult that you need skill and ability to do

A. Complete the conversations. Choose A, B or C.

Where did you go on vacation?

(a) Yes, I did. It was wonderful.
(b) I live in Seoul, Korea.
(c) I went to Jeju-do to see my grandparents.

1. Did you go there by airplane?

(a) Yes. It was very exciting.
(b) Wow! I've never taken an airplane.
(c) I had a part time job during vacation.

2. What did you do during the summer?

(a) No, I didn't. I climbed the mountain.
(b) I went to Jirisan with my family.
(c) Sounds great. Have a nice trip.

B. Where did you go on vacation? Write sentences as in the example.

1.

go to New York city

Q: Where did you go on vacation?

A: I _went to New York city._

2.

go to a camp about the earth

Q: Where did you go on vacation?

A: I _____

3.

go to a bicycle trip for three days

Q: Where did you go on vacation?

A: I _____

4.

visit many art museums

Q: Where did you go on vacation?

A: I _____

85

Super Writing 1

A. Look at the example. Make conversations as in the example.

1.

   `wonderful`   `go to Jeju-do`

   A: Did you have a good time last vacation?

   B: _Yes, I did. It was wonderful._

   A: What did you do?

   B: _I went to Jeju-do._

2.

   `amazing`   `make a trip to China for three days`

   A: Did you have a good time last vacation?

   B: _____

   A: What did you do?

   B: _____

3.

   `interesting`   `go to a concert with my girlfriend`

   A: Did you have a good time last vacation?

   B: _____

   A: What did you do?

   B: _____

4.

   `quite inspiring`   `go to a nursing home with my family`

   A: Did you have a good time last vacation?

   B: _____

   A: What did you do?

   B: _____

5.

   `fantastic`   `clean up the park with my friends`

   A: Did you have a good time last vacation?

   B: _____

   A: What did you do?

   B: _____

Super Writing 2

● 1~4 Unscramble the words to make sentences.
● 5~7 Sentence Transformation. / N(Negative) / Q(Question) / T(Tense)

1.

my grandparents | . | I | to see | went to Jeju-do

⇨ _____

2.

summer vacation | your | how | ? | was

⇨ _____

3.

in a small hotel | . | we | for five days | stayed

⇨ _____

4.

all the famous tourist sights | . | and the most famous museums | . | visited | we

⇨ _____

5.

He saw one of the most famous pictures in the world. (Q)

⇨ _____

6.

We had sandwiches for lunch in a park. (N)

⇨ _____

7.

We meet very interesting people. (T - Past)

⇨ _____

Super Speaking!

A. Listen to the dialog again. Please circle the correct words. ⊙ Track **94**

Suji: (a) How / (b) What   did you do this summer vacation, Eric?

Eric: I had a big a_____ with my father d_____ my summer vacation.

In the middle of summer, my father and I went on a bicycle trip

to Gangwon-do   (a) during / (b) for   three days.

Suji: Really? That sounds like a big c_____ .

Eric: It was. We   (a) rode / (b) ride   our bicycles all day and slept in a tent at night.

The weather was hot, and we had to go up and down a lot of hills.

Suji: Wow. How did you do it?

Eric: It was not easy, but I rode slowly and looked around at the trees, the rivers, and the

m_____ . I could feel nature and enjoy r_____ .

  (a) What / (b) How   was your summer vacation? Did you have fun?

Suji: I went to the a_____ p_____ with my cousins.

Eric: Really? That sounds really fun.

Suji: It was. We rode a roller coaster.

Eric: Wow. How was it?

Suji: It was s_____ at first, but I really enjoyed   (a) riding / (b) to ride   it.

We had a very wonderful time. It was an exciting vacation!

B. Let's Talk   Ask and answer the questions about the dialog with your partner.

1. What did the boy do during summer vacation?

⇨ He went _____ .

2. Where did the boy and his father sleep at night?

⇨ They _____ .

3. Where did Suji go with her cousins?

⇨ She went _____ .

Grammar Focus 1

● **One of the + Superlative + Plural Noun**

- We often say *one of the* before a superlative form. The noun that follows is plural.

Mt. Mckinley is one of the highest mountains in the world.

Training for the Olympics is one of the most difficult things for an athlete.

	One of	Superlative	Plural noun	
It is		the biggest	restaurants	in the city.
She is	one of	the prettiest	girls	in the class.
Seoul is		the most crowded	cities	in the world.

Grammar Focus 2

● **Gerund as Subject and Object**

- To form a gerund, we add *-ing* to the end of the verb. We can use a gerund like a noun. It can be the subject or the object of a sentence.

Flying in an airplane is not really dangerous.

Nancy loves her car and enjoys driving it.

- We can use a gerund as the object of certain verbs. Here are some of the verbs.

consider	keep on	finish	quit
discuss	give up	postpone	imagine
enjoy	keep	think about	(not) mind
dislike	put off	stop	start

A. Make sentences to describe the pictures as in the example. Use gerund subjects and objects.

1.

fish in a river / is relaxing for John

⇨ _Fishing in a river is relaxing for John._

2.

learn foreign languages / is interesting

⇨ _____

3.

walk alone at night / dangerous

⇨ _____

4.

Ann finished / study at night

⇨ _____

5.

I enjoy / take a walk along the lake

⇨ _____

6.

learn about other cultures / is really fun

⇨ _____

B. Write sentences using the prompts and *one of the* + superlative + plural noun.

1. The *Mona Lisa* / famous paintings / in the world

⇨ _The Mona Lisa is one of the most famous paintings in the world._

2. The Grand Canyon / beautiful places / in the world

⇨ _____

3. The Taj Mahal / beautiful buildings / in the world

⇨ _____

4. Gyeongbokgung / great historical sites / of Korea

⇨ _____

5. The Yangtze River / long rivers / in the world

⇨ _____

Building Vocabulary

A. Choose and fill in the blanks to make sentences.

violent	prevent	serious	fun
invented	communication	function	learn

1.

Don't you think watching TV is _____fun_____ for most people?

2.

People think that this movie is full of _____ scenes.

3.

Each button has a different _____.

4.

Edison _____ light bulb at the first setout.

5.

The school is improving _____ between teachers and parents.

6.

Students all across Asia work hard to _____ English.

7.

Most people agree that airbags save lives in _____ car accidents.

8.

The man is _____ people from entering.

91

B. Match the words and meanings. Draw a line between the word and its meaning.

WORD

MEANING

1.

change

•   • a. to find the answer to something

2.

lazy

•   • b. not wanting to work

3.

solve

•   • c. sad because something is not as good as you expected

4.

disappointed

•   • d. to make something different, or become different

C. Read the below sentences and choose the correct answers.

1. There *seems* to be a problem with the car. In this sentence *seems* means
   (a) to appear to be
   (b) to choose something or someone

2. My sister is studying *abroad*. In this sentence *abroad* menas
   (a) on or onto a ship or plane
   (b) in or to a foreign country

Super Exercise

A. Complete the two conversations. Choose (a), (b) or (c).

What kind of TV programs do you like?

(a) I like watching a reality show.
(b) I'm considering changing my job.
(c) You could watch it at my house.

1. What do you think of TV?

(a) I think TV is bad because it is too violent.

(b) That's a good idea.

(c) Well, I'm against it. It will take too much time.

2. Why are korean drams popular abroad?

(a) Korean Drama is famous and popular in the world.

(b) The reason why they are so popular is that the story of the drama is engaging and interesting.

(c) Watching them wastes time and they are useless.

B. How often do you watch TV? Answer the questions using the phrases in the boxes.

1.

| every day | American Idol |

Q: How often do you watch TV?
A: I watch TV every day.
Q: What's your favorite program?
A: My favorite program is American Idol.

2.

| three times a week | Running Man |

Q: How often do you watch TV?
A:
Q: What's your favorite program?
A:

3.

| Once a week | 2 Days 1 Night |

Q: How often do you watch TV?
A:
Q: What's your favorite program?
A:

4.

| twice a week | Six Flying Dragons |

Q: How often do you watch TV?
A:
Q: What's your favorite program?
A:

Super Writing 1

A. Look at the pictures. Complete the sentences using the phrases in the box.

doesn't like reality shows	likes a quiz show	don't like a documentary
doesn't like sports programs	like a cooking show	

1.

   ⇨ I think my mom   _doesn't like reality shows_

2.

   ⇨ I think she _____

3.

   ⇨ I think Peter and Jane _____

4.

   ⇨ I think they _____

5.

   ⇨ I think Jessica _____

B. Look at the example. Write sentences in the same way.

1. | bad | | too violent |

   ⇨   _I think TV is bad. Many programs are too violent._

2. | good | | exciting |

   ⇨ _____

3. | useful | | educational |

   ⇨ _____

● 1~4 Unscramble the words to make sentences.
● 5~7 Sentence Transformation. / N(Negative) / Q(Question) / T(Tense)

1.

| people's life | . | Television | has changed |

⇨ _____

2.

| through television | . | We | with many other people | can communicate |

⇨ _____

3.

| by watching TV | We | . | much knowledge | get |

⇨ _____

4.

| has created | . | as well | some serious problems | Television |

⇨ _____

5.

Watching too much TV is bad for eyes. (Q)

⇨ _____

6.

Television has great negative influence on children. (N)

⇨ _____

7.

They become lazy instead of going out. (T - Past)

⇨ _____

95

Super Speaking!

A. Read and repeat the dialog. Then use the speaking cards to practice it with your partner.

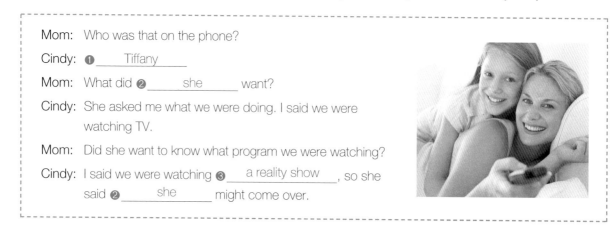

Mom: Who was that on the phone?

Cindy: ❶ ____Tiffany____

Mom: What did ❷ ____she____ want?

Cindy: She asked me what we were doing. I said we were watching TV.

Mom: Did she want to know what program we were watching?

Cindy: I said we were watching ❸ ___a reality show___, so she said ❷ ____she____ might come over.

❶ Eric
❷ he
❸ a sitcom

❶ Lucy
❷ she
❸ a police dram

B. What do you think? Complete the survey and then ask your partner.

TV Program	You	Your partner
1. quiz shows		
2. documentaries		
3. sitcoms		
4. cooking shows		
5. soap operas		
6. police dramas		
7. reality shows		
8. sports programs		

What do you think of sports programs?

I think sports programs are boring.

boring   violent   exciting

useful   educational   bad fir kinds

aterrible thing for children   fantastic

Grammar Focus

● The Conjunctions: *so* and *because*

- We use the conjunction *because* when we have to express a reason (say why something happens).

- We use the conjunction *so* to join each pair of sentences. The conjunction *so* is used to join alternative ideas. *So* shows that the second idea was the result of the first idea. The conjunction *so* shows cause-and-effect. Use a comma before the conjunction *so*.

Nancy didn't go to school because she is ill.   Susan didn't set her alarm, so she was late for school.

● The Present Perfect

- We form the present perfect of to be with *have* or *has* and the past participle of the verb to be.

- We use the present perfect for finished actions which have a connection to the present.

I have lost my keys!

(A finished action with a result in the present).

- We can use the present perfect to talk about an action or situation that started in the past and continues up to the present.

I've known Julie for ten years (and I still know her).

(Unfinished actions that started in the past and continue to the present)

- We use the present perfect for an action that has recently finished and its result is visible in the present.

Jane has washed her car.

(Jane's car was very dirty. Now it is clean.)

A. Complete the sentences with *so* or *because*. Add commas where necessary.

1. He has lost his glasses __, so__ he can't see anything.

2. All his friends have gone on holiday _____ he is very bored and doesn't know what to do.

3. We opened the window _____ it was very hot.

4. Linda is very hungry _____ she didn't have breakfast.

5. They had some free time _____ they went to the movies.

Super Speaking

• Look at the example and practice with a partner. Use the words below or invent your own. (Then change roles and practice again.)

you / see the Statue of Liberty?
⇨ No

Have you seen the Statue of Liberty?

No, I haven't. I didn't see the Statue of Liberty.

they / arrive in Seoul?
⇨ No

they / enjoy Seoul?
⇨ No

Clauida / eat good food?
⇨ No

they / buy tickets to a Broadway show?
⇨ No

you / see the 63 building
⇨ No

Answers

Unit 01

Building Vocabulary

A. 2. b   3. f   4. a   5. c   6. d

C. 1. c   2. d   3. a   4. b

D. 1. (a)   2. (b)

Super Exercise

A. 1. (a)   2. (b)   3. (a)   4. (c)

B. 1. two floors   2. four rooms

3. a living room and a kitchen, a bedroom

Super Writing 1

A. 2. Where is the cafeteria? / The cafeteria is on the second floor.

2. Where is the living room? / The living room is on the third floor.

3. Where is the seafood restaurant? / The seafood restaurant is on the fourth floor.

B. 2. There are math books under the bed.

3. There are golf clubs in my bedroom.

Super Writing 2

1. They met in 1997 at a charity soccer game.

2. The press named their house Beckingham Palace.

3. Where is my baseball cap?

4. Do you live in a house or an apartment?

5. You seemed to like your new house.

6. I didn't see the ghost in the dining room.

7. If you see a ghost in your home, what will you do?

Super Speaking!

A. 1. No, he doesn't. He lives in a house.

2. He had a barbecue party in the garden.

3. He saw it(the ghost) in the dining room.

Language Focus!

A. 2. Is there a telephone on the night table?

3. There aren't buses on the street.

4. Are there five floors in this building?

B. 2. No, she isn't. She is standing on the balcony.

3. No, he isn't. He is under the sea.

4. No, they aren't. They are in the school bus.

Unit 02

Building Vocabulary

A. 1. f, played soccer   2. d, watched TV

3. e, cleaned the house   4. g, went to the movies

6. b, traveled by plane   7. c, had delicious food

B. 1. went   2. got up   3. throw

C. 1. c   2. d   3. b   4. a

D. 1. (a)   2. (b)

Super Exercise

A. 2. David rode his bicycle last Saturday.

3. Sandra talked on the phone last Saturday.

4. David cleaned the house last Saturday.

B. 1. (c)   2. (b)

Super Writing 1

A. 2. Oh, I cleaned my room. / I went to the zoo.

3. Oh, I played tennis with my dad. / I went fishing at a lake.

B. 2. My grandfather cooked me *bulgogi* on Sunday afternoon.

3. Nancy studied Chinese on Sunday morning.

Super Writing 2

1. I ate breakfast and read a magazine.

2. I went to the Museum of Art History with my younger sister.

3. I was sorry that mom couldn't come with us.

4. I watched the latest action movie.

5. Did you have enough free time on the weekend?

6. Jessica listened to K-pop music yesterday.

7. Did you watch TV yesterday?

8. are you going to do this Saturday

Super Speaking!

A. 1. He went to the Museum of Art History with his sister.

2. Because she decided to visit Aunt Sophie, Uncle Daniel and her cousins Mark and Tina.

3. She had to practice for the competition and didn't have time to tour Rome with them.

4. She wrote an e-mail to her friends in England and read some comic books.

Language Focus!

A. 2. Did he enjoy his vacation? / he did

3. Did they like the film? / they didn't

4. Did it rain all day? / it did

5. Did you watch the discussion? / I didn't

B. 2. bought 3. drank 4. wore

Unit 03

Building Vocabulary

A. 2. blue 3. striped T-shirt 4. long brown 5. V-neck sweater 6. intelligent 7. thumb 8. similar

B. 2. FOREST 3. FACIAL 4. BREAK

C. 1. (a) 2. (b) 3. (a)

Super Exercise

A. 1. Ron Weasley 2. Dumbledore 3. Harry Potter 4. Hermione Granger 5. Professor Snape

B. 2. do, g 3. have, f 4. Is, a 5. does, c 6. Are, h 7. do, d 8. Does, b

Super Writing 1

A. 2. she's wearing a yellow striped shirt / he has long straight black hair

3. she's wearing a white blouse / she has black eyes

B. 2. curly brown hair / red sweater

3. long straight hair / checkered shirt

Super Writing 2

1. She has long blond hair and blue eyes.

2. She is wearing a green T-shirt.

3. Chimpanzees are closely related to humans.

4. You must exercise regularly.

5. Is he talking to the girl wearing a pair of glasses?

6. They used stones to break hard nuts.

7. She isn't cute and doesn't have curly brown hair.

Super Speaking!

A. 1. She exercises three times a week.

2. No, she doesn't. She has black curly hair.

3. She is talking to the man with moustache.

4. He is fat and bald. And he looks very old.

Language Focus!

A. 1. What, are 2. Where, is 3. Who, is

B. 2. Where are they 3. How are they 4. When is your

Unit 04

Building Vocabulary

A. 1. playing tennis 2. snowboarding 3. singing 4. cooking 5. inline skating 6. cycling 7. baker 8. skiing

B. 1. hobby 2. surf the Internet 3. go shopping

C. 1. b 2. d 3. a 4. c

D. 1. (a) 2. (a)

Super Exercise

A. 2. My favorite hobby is skateboarding.

3. My favorite hobby is playing the trumpet.

4. My favorite hobby is listening to music.

B. 2. When I have free time, I really enjoy going ice skating.

3. When I have free time, I really enjoy going fishing.

Super Writing 1

A. 2. going to go buying new clothes with Patricia this Sunday / have to finish my English class report

3. go bowling with George this Thursday / have to attend a seminar

B. 2. In the summer I spend a lot of time outdoors. When it is sunny I like going swimming. I also like watching a movie on TV with my father

3. In the summer I spend a lot of time outdoors, When it is sunny I like riding my bicycle. I also like listening to K-pop music with my friends

Super Writing 2

1. I'm not good at football or rugby.

2. She says that I'm really good at singing.

3. In the future I want to be a professional surfer.

4. Reading books helped me to gather much knowledge.

5. Does she have a pair of inline skates at home?

6. Karen doesn't like to sing in front of other people.

7. We're going to travel around the country.

Super Speaking!

A. 1. His favorite animation cartoon is Dooly.

2. Because the character is very cute.

3. Yes, she has.

4. They're going to go inline skating.

5. The parking lot in front of the skating rink.

Language Focus!

A. 2. to do, doing 3. to fight, fighting 4. to fly, flying

B. 2. Nancy wants to become a photographer.

3. Do you hope to travel by train?

4. Kevin promised not to bother her again.

Unit 05

Building Vocabulary

A. 1. horror movies 2. science fiction 3. writer

4. teenagers 5. translate 6. publishers 7. sell

8. hero

B. 1. c 2. d 3. b 4. a

C. 1. (a) 2. (b)

Super Exercise

A. 1. (c) 2. (a)

B. 2. My favorite type of movie is horror and comedy.

3. My favorite type of movie is romance.

4. My favorite type of movie is science fiction and adventure.

Super Writing 1

A. 2. Well, I can learn about cultures and languages. / I like action movies.

3. Well, I can learn about cultures and life styles. / I like romantic movies.

B. 2. My favorite movie is *Matrix*. It has great graphic quality and the story is exciting.

Super Writing 2

A. 1. J.K. Rowling is a very famous writer.

2. She went to a coffee shop to write the stories.

3. *Harry Potter* books became very popular for both children and adults.

4. Did you like a musical film?

5. Jessica has traveled by train.

6. Are Hollywood movies responsible for the behavior of today's youth?

7. I didn't see the movie *Finding Nemo*.

Super Speaking!

A. 1. She is a reporter for Film Magic Magazine

2. They go every Saturday

3. No, he doesn't. He likes horror movies.

4. Two free tickets for the movie theater.

Language Focus!

A. 2. Has, lost, has 3. Have, had, have 4. Have, seen, haven't 5. Have, called, have

B. 2. He has collected stamps since 2004.

3. They have worked for the company for ten years.

4. It has rained everywhere since last night.

Unit 06

Building Vocabulary

A. 1. cold and snowy 2. warm and sunny

3. hot and humid 4. windy and rainy

C. 1. Autumn 2. brightly 3. Numerous 4. thunderstorm

D. 1. (a) 2. (b) 3. (a) 4. (b)

Super Exercise

A. 1. (a) 2. (b) 3. (a) 4. (b) 5. (c)

Super Writing 1

A. 2. I'm going to go to Cairo. / It's hot and dry. / I think you should pack sunglasses.

3. I'm going to go to London. / It's windy and cold. / I think you should take a muffler and gloves.

B. 2. My favorite season is summer because I love to go camping. In summer, weather is warm and the sun shines throughout the day.

3. My favorite season is winter because I love to go skiing or snowboarding. In winter, weather is mostly cold and snowy.

Super Writing 2

1. Spring, summer, autumn, and winter are the four seasons of the year.

2. I don't have to wake up early and go to school.

3. Summer is the hottest season of the year.

4. Was there a lot of rain and strong winds?

5. Your moods changed with weather.

6. Many icebergs are melting because of global warming.

7. Is a cheetah the fastest animal in the world?

Language Focus!

A. 2. the smallest 3. the most beautiful 4. the longest

5. the fastest

B. 2. The giraffe is the tallest animal in the world.

3. The ostrich is the biggest bird in the world.

4. The Pluto is the farthest planet from the sun.

Unit 07

Building Vocabulary

A. 1. Dokdo 2. the Statue of Liberty 3. homework
4. during 5. nature 6. forget 7. cabin 8. campfire

B. 1. b 2. a 3. d 4. c

C. 1. (a) 2. (b)

Super Exercise

A. 1. (a) 2. (c)

B. 2. I'm traveling with my girlfriend.
3. I'm spending time with my friends.
4. I'm going to the beach.

Super Writing 1

A. 2. What are you doing next week? / I'm leaving my old apartment and I'm throwing a moving party.
3. What are you doing tonight? / I'm calling my family for a barbecue banquet.
4. What are you doing next Saturday? / I'm going to the beach with my family.

B. 2. We stayed at the farm for two weeks.
3. We stayed at the beach for three days.

Super Writing 2

1. My dad promised to go to Haeundae.
2. I'm going to help my mother with housework.
3. Do you have any special plans for this summer?
4. Who are you going to travel with?
5. Do schools, temples, or churches have special programs for this summer?
6. I'm going to visit Namsan hanok village.
7. The children stayed there four weeks and slept in tents or cabins.

Super Speaking!

A. 2. d 3. b 4. a

Language Focus!

A. 2. They are going to the movie theater.
3. She is playing tennis with her father.

B. 1. fascinating 2. boring 3. shocked 4. interesting

Unit 08

Building Vocabulary

A. 1. drive my car 2. walk to school 3. take the subway
4. catch the bus 5. ride my bicycle 6. take a taxi

B. 1. public transportation 2. safe 3. opportunity

C. 1. b 2. d 3. c 4. a

D. 1. (a) 2. (b) 3. (a)

Super Exercise

A. 1. (b) 2. (c)

B. 2. e 3. a 4. b 5. d

Super Writing 1

A. 2. How do you get to school? / Well, I usually take the subway. / How long does it take from home to school? / It takes about 10 minutes by subway.
3. How do you get to school? / Well, I usually walk. / How long does it take from home to school? / It takes about 15 minutes to walk.

B. 2. Bob takes the subway to work every day. It takes about fifteen minutes.
3. Jessica takes the(a) bus to work every day. It takes about forty minutes.

Super Writing 2

1. I ride my bicycle to school every day.
2. The subway is also widely used in some cities.
3. It also gives students opportunity to chat with their friends.
4. First, you need to buy a ticket to your destination.
5. I rode my bicycle to the subway station.
6. Should people stop using fossil fuels for transit and start using renewable energy sources?
7. Shakespeare didn't write these books.

Language Focus!

A. 2. wrote, written 3. painted, painted 4. grew, grown
5. visited, visited 6. stole, stolen 7. ate, eaten

B. 2. My laptop was stolen. 3. The room was cleaned by my mother. 4. That house was built in the middle ages.

Unit 09

Building Vocabulary

A. 1. Would you like to 2. a meal 3. wedding invitations
4. crowded 5. bedroom 6. soccer match 7. sent
8. go camping

B. 1. d 2. b 3. a 4. c

C. 1. (a) 2. (b)

Super Exercise

A. 1. Would you like to   2. Yes, I'd love to   3. How about you   4. Sorry, I can't

B. 1. 목요일로 생각하고 있어.   2. 시간나면, 함께 점심 먹는 게 어때?   3. 괜찮네.   4. 언제가 괜찮다고 생각하니? / 4 → 1 → 3

Super Writing 1

A. 2. Would you like to see a movie on Tuesday night? / I'd really like to, but I have to ask my mom first.
   3. Would you like to join us for dinner? / I'd really like to, but I have a project to do today.
   4. Would you like to go skiing this weekend? / I'd really like to, but I am going to a concert.

B. 2. we have to do our science project on Sunday night
   3. I have to practice the cello an hour every night

Super Writing 2

1. What are you doing to do this afternoon?
2. Sorry, I can't. I have to finish my school project.
3. I've promised to go to the movie theater with my sister.
4. In Britain, people often invite friends for a meal.
5. Is it Kathy's birthday next week?
6. There were 15 people staying at our house.
7. Let's not go out for a meal.

Language Focus!

A. 2. Let's go to a baseball game.   3. Let's leave at six-thirty.   4. Let's eat out for dinner.   5. Let's send Harry an e-mail.

B. 3. Would you like   4. Do you like   5. Do you like
   6. Would you like

Unit 10

Building Vocabulary

A. 1. Go straight   2. cross the street   3. neighborhood
   4. quiet   5. dry cleaner's   6. hair salon   7. amusement park   8. flower shop

B. 1. c   2. a   3. b   4. d

C. 1. (a)   2. (b)

Super Exercise

A. 1. T   2. F   3. T   4. T   5. F
   The school is next to the car park. / The supermarket is across from the park

B. 1. There is   2. There are   3. There are   4. There is
   5. There is   6. There are

Super Writing 1

A. 2. Excuse me. I'm looking for the movie theater on this map. / Yes. Go straight for one block and turn right. It's next to the bank.
   3. Excuse me. I'm looking for the bookstore on this map. / Yes. Go straight two blocks and turn left. It's across from the library.
   4. Excuse me. I'm looking for the bakery on this map. / Yes. Go straight one block and turn left. It's in front of the library.
   5. Excuse me. I'm looking for the post office on this map. / Yes. Go straight two blocks and turn right. It's next to the school.

Super Writing 2

1. I have lived in my perfect neighborhood for five years.
2. My house is between a big park and a post office.
3. On the weekend I sometimes jog in the park with my dad
4. I need to take two buses to get to school.
5. Is there a bookstore where students can buy their textbooks?
6. In fact, I needed about 10 minutes walk to the bus stop.
7. The restaurant isn't between the shoe shop and the post office.

Super Speaking!

A. so, (m)ovie (t)heater, (b)locks, right, How, (f)ar, (n)ext to, about, When, (a)ncient, (a)mazing , (s)imilar, different

B. 1. in the city is nearby
   2. for two blocks and turn right at the corner
   3. for one block, turn left at the corner
   4. take about 5 minutes

Language Focus!

A. 2. At the bus stop.   3. At the airport.   4. On the wall.
   5. In the bus.   6. On the table.

B. 2. next to/by   3. in front of/near   4. between, and

Unit 11

Building Vocabulary

A. 1. vacation   2. grandparents   3. airplane   4. cheap
   5. tourist sight   6. impressed   7. taking a photo
   8. interesting

B. 1. c   2. a   3. d   4. b

C. 1. (a)   2. (b)

Super Exercise

A. 1. (a)   2. (b)

B. 2. I went to a camp about the earth.

   3. I went to a bicycle trip for three days.

   4. I visited many art museums.

Super Writing 1

A. 2. Yes, I did. It was amazing. / I made a trip to China for three days.

   2. Yes, I did. It was interesting. / I went to a concert with my girlfriend.

   4. Yes, I did. It was quite inspiring. / I went to a nursing home with my family

   5. Yes, I did. It was fantastic. / I cleaned up the park with my friends.

Super Writing 2

1. I went to Jeju-do to see my grandparents.

2. How was your summer vacation?

3. We stayed for five days in a small hotel.

4. We visited all the famous tourist sights and the most famous museums.

5. Did he see one of the most famous pictures in the world?

6. We didn't have sandwiches for lunch in a park.

7. We met very interesting people.

Super Speaking!

A. What, (a)dventure, (d)uring, for, (c)hallenge, rode, (m)ountains, (r)iding, How, (a)musement (p)ark, (s)cary, riding

B. 1. on a bicycle trip with his father to Gangwon-do for three days.

   2. slept in a tent at night.

   3. to the amusement park with her cousins.

Language Focus!

A. 2. Learning foreign languages is interesting.

   3. Walking alone at night is dangerous.

   4. Ann finished studying at night.

   5. I enjoy taking a walk along the lake.

   6. Learning about other cultures is really fun.

B. 2. The Grand Canyon is one of the most beautiful places in the world.

   3. The Taj Mahal is one of the most beautiful buildings in the world.

   4. Gyeongbokgung is one of the greatest historical sites of Korea.

   5. The Yangtze River is one of the longest rivers in the world.

Unit 12

Building Vocabulary

A. 2. violent   3. function   4. invented   5. communication
   6. learn   7. serious   8. preventing

B. 1. d   2. b   3. a   4. c

C. 1. (a)   2. (b)

Super Exercise

A. 2. (a)   3. (b)

B. 2. I watch TV three times a week. / My favorite program is Running Man.

   3. I watch TV once a week. / My favorite program is 2 Days 1 Night.

   4. I watch TV twice a week. / My favorite program is Six Flying Dragons.

Super Writing 1

A. 2. likes a quiz show   3. like a cooking show   4. don't like a documentary   5. doesn't like sports programs

B. 2. I think TV is good. Many programs are exciting.

   3. I think TV is useful. Many programs are educational.

Super Writing 2

1. Television has changed people's life.

2. We can communicate with many other people through television.

3. We get much knowledge by watching TV.

4. Television has created some serious problems as wel.

5. Is watching too much TV bad for eyes?

6. Television doesn't have great negative influence on children.

7. They became lazy instead of going out.

Language Focus!

A. 2. , so   3. because   4. because   5. , so